I0448407

Congressional Research Service

Informing the legislative debate since 1914

Internet Governance and the Domain Name System: Issues for Congress

Lennard G. Kruger

Specialist in Science and Technology Policy

May 23, 2014

Congressional Research Service

7-5700

www.crs.gov

R42351

Summary

The Internet is often described as a "network of networks" because it is not a single physical entity, but hundreds of thousands of interconnected networks linking hundreds of millions of computers around the world. As such, the Internet is international, decentralized, and comprised of networks and infrastructure largely owned and operated by private sector entities. As the Internet grows and becomes more pervasive in all aspects of modern society, the question of how it should be governed becomes more pressing.

Currently, an important aspect of the Internet is governed by a private sector, international organization called the Internet Corporation for Assigned Names and Numbers (ICANN), which manages and oversees some of the critical technical underpinnings of the Internet such as the domain name system and Internet Protocol (IP) addressing. ICANN makes its policy decisions using a multistakeholder model of governance, in which a "bottom-up" collaborative process is open to all constituencies of Internet stakeholders.

National governments have recognized an increasing stake in ICANN policy decisions, especially in cases where Internet policy intersects with national laws addressing such issues as intellectual property, privacy, law enforcement, and cybersecurity. Some governments around the world are advocating increased intergovernmental influence over the way the Internet is governed. For example, specific proposals have been advanced that would create an Internet governance entity within the United Nations (U.N.). Other governments (including the United States), as well as many other Internet stakeholders, oppose these proposals and argue that ICANN's multistakeholder model is the most appropriate way to govern the Internet. On May 14, 2013, H.R. 1580, which states that "it is the policy of the United States to preserve and advance the successful multistakeholder model that governs the Internet" was passed unanimously by the House.

Currently, the U.S. government, through the National Telecommunications and Information Administration (NTIA) at the Department of Commerce, holds a "stewardship" role over the domain name system by virtue of a contractual relationship with ICANN. On March 14, 2014, NTIA announced its intention to transition its stewardship role and procedural authority over key domain name functions to the global Internet multistakeholder community. If a satisfactory transition can be achieved, NTIA will let its contract with ICANN expire on September 30, 2015. NTIA has stated that it will not accept any transition proposal that would replace the NTIA role with a government-led or an intergovernmental organization solution.

Congress is likely to closely examine NTIA's proposed transition of its authority over ICANN. As a transition plan is developed by ICANN and the Internet community, Congress will likely monitor and evaluate that plan, and seek assurances that an Internet and domain name system free of U.S. government stewardship will remain stable, secure, resilient, and open. Meanwhile, Congress will likely continue assessing to what extent ongoing and future intergovernmental telecommunications conferences constitute an opportunity for some nations to increase intergovernmental control over the Internet, and how effectively NTIA and other government agencies (such as the State Department) are working to counteract that threat.

Meanwhile, H.R. 4342 (the DOTCOM Act) was approved by the House Energy and Commerce Committee on May 8, 2014, to prohibit the NTIA from relinquishing responsibility over the Internet domain name system until the Government Accountability Office (GAO) submits a report to Congress examining the ramifications of the proposed transfer. The language of H.R. 4342 was successfully added as an amendment to H.R. 4435, the FY2015 National Defense

Authorization Act, which was passed by the House on May 22, 2014. Other bills introduced into the 113th Congress (H.R. 4367 and H.R. 4398) would also place limits on NTIA's ability to transfer its authority over certain domain name functions.

Contents

Figures

Appendixes

Contacts

What Is Internet Governance?

There is no universally agreed-upon definition of "Internet governance." A more limited definition would encompass the management and coordination of the technical underpinnings of the Internet—such as domain names, addresses, standards, and protocols that enable the Internet to function. A broader definition would include the many factors that shape a variety of Internet policy-related issues, such as such as intellectual property, privacy, Internet freedom, e-commerce, and cybersecurity.

One working definition was developed at the World Summit on the Information Society (WSIS) in 2005:

> Internet governance is the development and application by governments, the private sector and civil society, in their respective roles, of shared principles, norms, rules, decision-making procedures, and programmes that shape the evolution and use of the Internet.[1]

Another definition developed by the Internet Governance Project (IGP)[2] delineates three aspects of the Internet that may require some level of governing: *technical standardization*, which involves arriving at and agreeing upon technical standards and protocols; *resource allocation and assignment*, which includes domain names and Internet Protocol (IP) addresses; and *human conduct on the Internet*, encompassing the regulations, rules, and policies affecting areas such as spam, cybercrime, copyright and trademark disputes, consumer protection issues, and public and private security. With these three categories in mind, the IGP definition is:

> Internet governance is collective decisionmaking by owners, operators, developers, and users of the networks connected by Internet protocols to establish policies, rules, and dispute resolution procedures about technical standards, resource allocations, and/or the conduct of people engaged in global internetworking activities.[3]

How Is the Internet Currently Governed?

The nature of the Internet, with its decentralized architecture and structure, makes the practice of governing a complex proposition. First, the Internet is inherently international and cannot in its totality be governed by national governments whose authority ends at national borders. Second, the Internet's successful functioning depends on the willing cooperation and participation by mostly private sector stakeholders around the world. These stakeholders include owners and operators of servers and networks around the world, domain name registrars and registries, regional IP address allocation organizations, standards organizations, Internet service providers, and Internet users.

---

[1] Tunis Agenda for the Information Society, November 18, 2005, WSIS-05/TUNIS/DOC6(Rev.1)-E, p. 6, available at http://www.itu.int/wsis/docs2/tunis/off/6rev1.pdf.

[2] The IGP describes itself as "an alliance of academics that puts expertise into practical action in the fields of global governance, Internet policy, and information and communication technology." See http://www.internetgovernance.org.

[3] Milton Mueller, John Mathiason, and Hans Klein, "The Internet and Global Governance: Principles and Norms for a New Regime," *Global Governance*, vol. 13 (2007), p. 245.

Given the multiplicity and diversity of Internet stakeholders, a number of organizations and entities play varying roles. It is important to note that all of the Internet stakeholders cited above participate in various ways within the various fora, organizations, and frameworks addressing Internet governance and policy.

Key organizations in the private sector include the following:

Internet Corporation for Assigned Names and Numbers (ICANN)—ICANN was created in 1998 through a Memorandum of Understanding with the Department of Commerce (see the following section of this report, "Role of U.S. Government"). Directed by an internationally constituted Board of Directors, ICANN is a private, not-for-profit organization based in Marina Del Ray, CA, which manages and oversees the critical technical underpinnings of the Internet such as the domain name system (DNS) and IP addressing (see the **Appendix** for more background information on ICANN). ICANN implements and enforces many of its policies and rules through contracts with *registries* (companies and organizations who operate and administer the master database of all domain names registered in each top level domain, such as .com and .org) and accredited *registrars* (the hundreds of companies and organizations with which consumers register domain names). Policies are developed by Supporting Organizations and Committees in a consensus-based "bottom-up" process open to various constituencies and stakeholders of the Internet. As such, ICANN is often pointed to as emblematic of the "multistakeholder model" of Internet governance.

Internet standards organizations—As the Internet has evolved, groups of engineers, researchers, users, and other interested parties have coalesced to develop technical standards and protocols necessary to enable the Internet to function smoothly. These organizations conduct standards development processes that are open to participants and volunteers from around the world. Internet standards organizations include the Internet Engineering Task Force (IETF), the Internet Architecture Board (IAB), the Internet Society (ISOC), and the World Wide Web Consortium (W3C).

Governmental entities involved in Internet governance include the following:

Governmental Advisory Committee (GAC)—As part of ICANN's multistakeholder process, the GAC provides advice to the ICANN Board on matters of public policy, especially in cases where ICANN activities and policies may interact with national laws or international agreements related to issues such as intellectual property, law enforcement, and privacy. Although the ICANN Board is required to consider GAC advice and recommendations, it is not obligated to follow those recommendations. Membership in the GAC is open to all national governments who wish to participate. Currently, there are 113 nations represented, and the GAC Chair is presently held by Canada, with Vice Chairs held by Kenya, Sweden, and Singapore.

Internet Governance Forum (IGF)—The IGF was established in 2006 by the United Nation's World Summit on the Information Society (WSIS). The purpose of the IGF is to provide a multistakeholder forum which provides an open discussion (in yearly meetings) on public policies related to the Internet. Open to all stakeholders and interested parties (governments, industry, academia, civil society), the IGF serves as an open discussion forum and does not have negotiated outcomes, nor does it make formal recommendations to the U.N. In December 2010, the U.N. General Assembly renewed the IGF through 2015 and tasked the U.N.'s Commission on Science and Technology for Development (CSTD) to develop a report and recommendations on how the IGF might be improved. A Working Group on Improvements to the Internet Governance Forum was formed by the U.N., which includes 22 governments (including the United States) and the participation of Internet stakeholder groups.

Other International Organizations—Other existing international organizations address Internet policy issues in various ways. The International Telecommunications Union (ITU) is the United Nations' specialized agency for communications and information technology. The World Intellectual Property Organization (WIPO) is another specialized agency of the U.N., which addresses a wide range of intellectual property issues, including those related to Internet policy. The Organisation for Economic Co-operation and Development (OECD) provides a forum for governments to work together to address economic issues, including the recent development of Internet policymaking principles. While none of these organizations have direct control or authority over the Internet, their activities can have influence over future directions of global Internet policy.

National governments—National governments have acted to address various Internet policy issues within their own borders. Many of the national laws and regulations pertain to user behavior on the Internet. For example, in the United States, laws have been passed addressing such issues as cybersecurity and cybercrime, Internet gambling, Internet privacy, and protection of intellectual property on the Internet. Governments have also established internal Internet policy coordinating bodies (e.g., the National Telecommunications and Information Administration's Internet Policy Task Force and the European Commission's Information Society).

Role of U.S. Government

The United States government has no statutory authority over ICANN or the domain name system. However, because the Internet evolved from a network infrastructure created by the Department of Defense, the U.S. government originally owned and operated (primarily through private contractors) many of the key components of network architecture that enabled the domain name system to function. In the early 1990s, the National Science Foundation (NSF) was given a lead role in overseeing domain names used in the civilian portion of the Internet (which at that time was largely comprised of research universities). By the late 1990s, ICANN was created, the Internet had expanded into the commercial world, and the National Telecommunications and Information Administration (NTIA) of the Department of Commerce (DOC) assumed the lead role.

A 1998 Memorandum of Understanding between ICANN and the DOC initiated a process intended to transition technical DNS coordination and management functions to a private-sector not-for-profit entity. While the DOC plays no role in the internal governance or day-to-day operations of ICANN, the U.S. government, through the DOC/NTIA, retains a role with respect to the DNS via three separate contractual agreements. These are:

- a 2009 Affirmation of Commitments (AoC) between DOC and ICANN;[4]

---

[4] For more information on the Affirmation of Commitments, including the precursor agreements between DOC and ICANN such as the Joint Project Agreement and the Memorandum of Understanding, see CRS Report 97-868, *Internet Domain Names: Background and Policy Issues*, by Lennard G. Kruger.

- a contract between ICANN and DOC to perform various technical functions such as allocating IP address blocks, editing the root zone file, and coordinating the assignment of unique protocol numbers; and

- a cooperative agreement between DOC and VeriSign to manage and maintain the official DNS root zone file.

By virtue of those three contractual agreements, the United States government—through DOC/NTIA—exerts a legacy authority and stewardship over ICANN, and arguably has more influence over ICANN and the DNS than other national governments.

While NTIA is the lead agency overseeing domain name issues, other federal agencies maintain a specific interest in the DNS that may affect their particular missions. For example, the Federal Trade Commission (FTC) seeks to protect consumer privacy on the Internet, the Department of Justice (DOJ) addresses Internet crime and intellectual property issues, and the Department of Defense and Department of Homeland Security address cybersecurity issues. However, none of these agencies have legal authority over ICANN or the running of the DNS.

Affirmation of Commitments

On September 30, 2009, DOC and ICANN announced agreement on an Affirmation of Commitments (AoC) to "institutionalize and memorialize" the technical coordination of the DNS globally and by a private-sector-led organization.[5] The AoC replaced the previous Memorandum of Understanding and subsequent Joint Project Agreement between DOC and ICANN. It has no expiration date and would conclude only if one of the two parties decided to terminate the agreement.

Under the AoC, ICANN committed to remain a not-for-profit corporation "headquartered in the United States of America with offices around the world to meet the needs of a global community." According to the AoC, "ICANN is a private organization and nothing in this Affirmation should be construed as control by any one entity." Specifically, the AoC called for the establishment of review panels which will periodically make recommendations to the ICANN Board in four areas: ensuring accountability, transparency, and the interests of global Internet users (panel includes the Administrator of NTIA); preserving security, stability, and resiliency; impact of new generic top level domains (gTLDs); and WHOIS policy.[6]

On December 31, 2010, the Accountability and Transparency Review Team (ATRT) released its recommendations to the Board for improving ICANN's transparency and accountability with respect to Board governance and performance, the role and effectiveness of the GAC and its interaction with the Board, public input and policy development processes, and review mechanisms for Board decisions.[7] At the June 2011 meeting in Singapore, the Board adopted all

---

[5] Affirmation of Commitments by the United States Department of Commerce and the Internet Corporation for Assigned Names and Numbers, September 30, 2009, available at http://www.ntia.doc.gov/ntiahome/domainname/ Affirmation_of_Commitments_2009.pdf.

[6] WHOIS is a publically available online database that provides information on domain name registrants. WHOIS is used to identify domain name holders. WHOIS policy is controversial because it encompasses two competing considerations: protecting the privacy of domain name holders versus enabling law enforcement and trademark holders to identify owners of domain names and websites engaging in criminal activities or infringing on intellectual property.

[7] The ATRT final report is available at http://www.icann.org/en/reviews/affirmation/atrt-final-recommendations-
(continued...)

27 ATRT recommendations. According to NTIA, "the focus turns to ICANN management and staff, who must take up the challenge of implementing these recommendations as rapidly as possible and in a manner that leads to meaningful and lasting reform."[8]

DOC Contract and Cooperative Agreement With ICANN and VeriSign

A contract between DOC and ICANN—specifically referred to as the "IANA[9] functions contract"—authorizes ICANN to manage the technical underpinnings of the DNS. Specifically, the contract allows ICANN to perform various critical technical functions such as allocating IP address blocks, editing the root zone file, and coordinating the assignment of unique protocol numbers. Additionally, and intertwined with the IANA functions, a cooperative agreement between DOC and VeriSign (the company that operates the .com and .net registries) authorizes VeriSign to manage and maintain the official root zone file that is contained in the Internet's root servers that underlie the functioning of the DNS.[10] By virtue of these legal agreements, the DOC approves changes or modifications made to the root zone file (changes, for example, such as adding a new top level domain).[11]

On July 2, 2012, NTIA announced the award of the most recent (and current) IANA contract to ICANN through September 30, 2015 (with an option to extend the contract through September 2019). The IANA contract continues to specify that the contractor must be a wholly U.S. owned and operated firm or a U.S. university or college; that all primary operations and systems shall remain within the United States; and that the U.S. government reserves the right to inspect the premises, systems, and processes of all facilities and components used for the performance of the contract.

(...continued)

31dec10-en.pdf.

[8] NTIA, *Press Release*, "NTIA Commends ICANN Board on Adopting the Recommendations of the Accountability and Transparency Review Team," June 24, 2011, available at http://www.ntia.doc.gov/press/2011/NTIA_Statement_06242011.html.

[9] Internet Assigned Numbers Authority.

[10] According to the National Research Council, "The root zone file defines the DNS. For all practical purposes, a top level domain (and, therefore, all of its lower-level domains) is in the DNS if and only if it is listed in the root zone file. Therefore, presence in the root determines which DNS domains are available on the Internet." See National Research Council, Committee on Internet Navigation and the Domain Name System, *Technical Alternatives and Policy Implications, Signposts on Cyberspace: The Domain Name System and Internet Navigation*, National Academy Press, Washington, DC, 2005, p. 97.

[11] The June 30, 2005, "U.S. Principles on the Internet's Domain Name and Addressing System" stated the intention to "preserve the security and stability" of the DNS, and asserted that "the United States is committed to taking no action that would have the potential to adversely impact the effective and efficient operation of the DNS and will therefore maintain its historic role in authorizing changes or modifications to the authoritative root zone file." See http://www.ntia.doc.gov/ntiahome/domainname/USDNSprinciples_06302005.pdf.

NTIA Intent to Transition Stewardship of the DNS

The IANA functions contract with ICANN and the cooperative agreement with Verisign give NTIA the authority to maintain a stewardship and oversight role with respect to ICANN and the domain name system. On March 14, 2014, NTIA announced its intention to transition its stewardship role and procedural authority over key domain name functions to the global Internet multistakeholder community.[12] If a satisfactory transition can be achieved, NTIA will let its IANA functions contract with ICANN expire on September 30, 2015.

As a first step, NTIA is asking ICANN to convene interested global Internet stakeholders (both from the private sector and governments) to develop a proposal to achieve the transition. Specifically, NTIA expects ICANN to work collaboratively with parties directly affected by the IANA contract, including the Internet Engineering Task Force (IETF), the Internet Architecture Board (IAB), the Internet Society (ISOC), the Regional Internet Registries (RIRs), top level domain name operators, Verisign, and other interested global stakeholders. In October 2013, many of these groups—specifically, the Internet technical organizations responsible for coordination of the Internet infrastructure—had called for "accelerating the globalization of ICANN and IANA functions, towards an environment in which all stakeholders, including all governments, participate on an equal footing."[13]

NTIA has stated that it will not accept any transition proposal that would replace the NTIA role with a government-led or an intergovernmental organization solution.

In addition, NTIA told ICANN that the transition proposal must have broad community support and address the following four principles:

- support and enhance the multistakeholder model;

- maintain the security, stability, and resilience of the Internet DNS;

- meet the needs and expectation of the global customers and partners of the IANA services; and

- maintain the openness of the Internet.

Supporters of the transition[14] argue that by transferring its remaining authority over ICANN and the DNS to the global Internet community, the U.S. government will bolster its continuing support for the multistakeholder model of Internet governance, and that this will enable the United States to more effectively argue and work against proposals for intergovernmental control over the Internet. Supporters also point out that the U.S. government and Internet stakeholders have, from the inception of ICANN, envisioned that U.S. authority over IANA functions would be temporary, and that the DNS would eventually be completely privatized.[15] According to NTIA,

---

[12] NTIA, *Press Release*, "NTIA Announced Intent to Transition Key Internet Domain Name Functions," March 14, 2014, available at http://www ntia.doc.gov/press-release/2014/ntia-announces-intent-transition-key-internet-domain-name-functions.

[13] ICANN, "Montevideo Statement on the Future of Internet Cooperation," October 7, 2013, available at https://www.icann.org/en/news/announcements/announcement-07oct13-en htm.

[14] ICANN, "Endorsements of the IANA Globalization Process," March 18, 2014, available at https://www.icann.org/en/about/agreements/iana/globalization-endorsements-18mar14-en.pdf.

[15] The Commerce Department's June 10, 1998 Statement of Policy stated that the U.S. government "is committed to a transition that will allow the private sector to take leadership for DNS management." Available at (continued...)

this transition is now possible, given that "ICANN as an organization has matured and taken steps in recent years to improve its accountability and transparency and its technical competence."[16]

Those opposed, skeptical, or highly cautious about the transition[17] point out that NTIA's role has served as a necessary "backstop" which has given Internet stakeholders confidence that the integrity and stability of the DNS is being sufficiently overseen. Critics assert that in the wake of the Edward Snowden NSA revelations, foreign governments might gain more support internationally in their continuing attempts to exert intergovernmental control over the Internet, and that any added intergovernmental influence over the Internet and the DNS would be that much more detrimental to the interests of the United States if NTIA's authority over ICANN and the DNS were to no longer exist. Another concern regards the development of the transition plan and a new international multistakeholder entity that would provide some level of stewardship over the domain name system. Critics are concerned about the risks of foreign governments—particularly those favoring censorship of the Internet—gaining influence over the DNS through the transition to a new Internet governance mechanism that no longer is subject to U.S. government oversight.

Legislative Activities

On March 27, 2014, Representative Shimkus introduced H.R. 4342, the Domain Openness Through Continued Oversight Matters (DOTCOM) Act. H.R. 4342 would prohibit the NTIA from relinquishing responsibility over the Internet domain name system until GAO submits to Congress a report on the role of the NTIA with respect to such system. The report would include a discussion and analysis of the advantages and disadvantages of the change and address the national security concerns raised by relinquishing U.S. oversight. It would also require GAO to provide a definition of the term "multistakeholder model" as used by NTIA with respect to Internet policymaking and governance. H.R. 4342 was referred to the House Energy and Commerce Committee. On April 2, 2014, the Subcommittee on Communications and Technology held a hearing on the DOTCOM Act.[18] H.R. 4342 was approved by the House Energy and Commerce Committee on May 8, 2014.

On May 22, 2014, the text of the DOTCOM Act was offered by Representative Shimkus as an amendment to H.R. 4435, the National Defense Authorization Act for FY2015. During House consideration of H.R. 4435, the amendment was agreed to by a vote of 245-177. H.R. 4435 was passed by the House on May 22, 2014. The House Armed Services bill report accompanying H.R. 4435 (H.Rept. 113-446) stated the Committee's belief that any new Internet governance structure should include protections for the Department of Defense-controlled .mil generic top level

---

(...continued)

http://www.ntia.doc.gov/legacy/ntiahome/domainname/6_5_98dns.htm.

[16] NTIA, *Press Release*, "NTIA Announced Intent to Transition Key Internet Domain Name Functions," March 14, 2014

[17] See for example: Atkinson, Rob, "U.S. Giving Up Its Internet 'Bodyguard' Role," March 17, 2014, available at http://www.ideaslaboratory.com/2014/03/17/u-s-giving-up-its-internet-bodyguard-role/; and Nagesh, Gauthem, *Wall Street Journal*, "U.S. Plan for Web Faces Credibility Issue," March 18, 2014.

[18] Hearing before the House Energy and Commerce Committee, Subcommittee on Communications and Technology, "Ensuring the Security, Stability, Resilience, and Freedom of the Global Internet," April 2, 2014, available at http://energycommerce.house.gov/hearing/ensuring-security-stability-resilience-and-freedom-global-internet.

domain and its associated Internet protocol numbers. The Committee also supported maintaining separation between the policymaking and technical operation of root-zone management functions.

Meanwhile, the Senate Armed Services Committee, in its May 23 markup of the National Defense Authorization Act, included sense of the Senate language stating that "the Secretary of Defense should advise the President not to transfer the U.S. Government's role in Internet governance unless he is confident that the .mil top-level domain and Internet Protocol address numbers used exclusively by the Department of Defense for national security will remain exclusively used by the Department of Defense."[19]

On May 8, 2014, the House Appropriations Committee approved the FY2015 Commerce, Justice, Science (CJS) Appropriations bill, which appropriates funds for DOC and NTIA. The bill report states that in order that the transition be more fully considered by Congress, the Committee's recommendation for NTIA does not include any funds to carry out the transition and that the Committee expects that NTIA will maintain the existing no-cost contract with ICANN throughout FY2015.

Other legislation addressing the proposed transition includes H.R. 4367 (Internet Stewardship Act of 2014, introduced by Representative Mike Kelly on April 2, 2014), which would prohibit NTIA from relinquishing its DNS responsibilities unless permitted by statute; and H.R. 4398 (Global Internet Freedom Act of 2014, introduced by Representative Duffy on April 4, 2014) which would prohibit NTIA from relinquishing its authority over the IANA functions. Both H.R. 4367 and H.R. 4398 were referred to the Committee on Energy and Commerce. Meanwhile, the House Judiciary Committee, Subcommittee on Courts, Intellectual Property, and the Internet, held a hearing on April 10, 2014, that examined the proposed transition.

Multistakeholder Process to Develop a Transition Proposal

ICANN has begun to convene a process through which the multistakeholder community will attempt to come to consensus on a transition proposal. Based on feedback received from the Internet community at its March 2014 meeting in Singapore, ICANN has put out for public input and comment a draft proposal of *Principles, Mechanisms and Process to Develop a Proposal to Transition NTIA's Stewardship of the IANA Functions.*[20] Under the draft proposal, a steering group would be formed "to steward the process in an open, transparent, inclusive, and accountable manner."[21] The steering group would be composed of representatives of each ICANN constituency and of parties directly affected by the transition of IANA functions (for example, Internet standards groups and Internet number resource organizations).

Debate over Future Model of Internet Governance

Given its complexity, diversity, and international nature, how should the Internet be governed? Some assert that a multistakeholder model of governance is appropriate, where all stakeholders

---

[19] Available at http://www.armed-services.senate.gov/imo/media/doc/SASC%20NDAA%20markup%20release%2005-23-14.pdf.

[20] Available at http://www.icann.org/en/about/agreements/iana/transition/draft-proposal-08apr14-en.htm.

[21] Ibid.

(both public and private sectors) arrive at consensus through a transparent bottom-up process. Others argue that a greater role for national governments is necessary, either through increased influence through the multistakeholder model, or under the auspices of an international body exerting intergovernmental control.

To date, ICANN and the governance of the domain name system has been the focal point of this debate. While ICANN's mandate is to manage portions of the technical infrastructure of the Internet (domain names and IP addresses), many of the decisions ICANN makes affect other aspects of Internet policy, including areas such as intellectual property, privacy, and cybersecurity. These are areas which many national governments have addressed for their own citizens and constituencies through domestic legislation, as well as through international treaties.

As part of the debate over an appropriate model of Internet governance, criticisms of ICANN have arisen on two fronts. One criticism reflects the tension between national governments and the current performance and governance processes of ICANN, whereby governments feel they lack adequate influence over ICANN decisions that affect a range of Internet policy issues. The other criticism is fueled by concerns of many nations that the U.S. government holds undue legacy influence and control over ICANN and the domain name system.

The debate over multistakeholderism vs. intergovernmental control initially manifested itself in 2005 at the World Summit on the Information Society (WSIS), which was a conference organized by the United Nations. More recently, this debate has been rekindled in various international fora, partially sparked by two ICANN actions in 2011: the approval of the .xxx top-level domain and the approval of a process to allow an indefinite number of new generic top level domains (gTLDs).

2005 World Summit on the Information Society (WSIS)

Following the creation of ICANN in 1998, many in the international community, including foreign governments, argued that it was inappropriate for the U.S. government to maintain its legacy authority over ICANN and the DNS. They suggested that management of the DNS should be accountable to a higher intergovernmental body. The United Nations, at the first phase of the WSIS in December 2003, debated and agreed to study the issue of how to achieve greater international involvement in the governance of the Internet, and the domain name system in particular. The study was conducted by the U.N.'s Working Group on Internet Governance (WGIG). On July 14, 2005, the WGIG released its report,[22] stating that no single government should have a preeminent role in relation to international Internet governance. The report called for further internationalization of Internet governance, and proposed the creation of a new global forum for Internet stakeholders. Four possible models were put forth, including two involving the creation of new Internet governance bodies linked to the U.N. Under three of the four models, ICANN would either be supplanted or made accountable to a higher intergovernmental body. The report's conclusions were scheduled to be considered during the second phase of the WSIS held in Tunis in November 2005. U.S. officials stated their opposition to transferring control and administration of the domain name system from ICANN to any international body. Similarly, the

---

[22] Working Group on Internet Governance, Report from the Working Group on Internet Governance, World Summit on the Information Society, Document WSIS-II/PC-3/DOC/5-E, August 3, 2005, available at http://www.itu.int/wsis/docs2/pc3/html/off5/index.html.

109th Congress expressed its support for maintaining existing U.S. control over ICANN and the DNS (H.Con.Res. 268 and S.Res. 323).[23]

The European Union (EU) initially supported the U.S. position. However, during the September 2005 preparatory meetings, the EU seemingly shifted its support towards an approach which favored an enhanced international role in governing the Internet. Conflict at the WSIS Tunis Summit over control of the domain name system was averted by the announcement, on November 15, 2005, of an Internet governance agreement between the United States, the EU, and over 100 other nations. Under this agreement, ICANN and the United States maintained their roles with respect to the domain name system. A new international group under the auspices of the U.N. was formed—the Internet Governance Forum (IGF)—which would provide an ongoing forum for all stakeholders (both governments and nongovernmental groups) to discuss and debate Internet policy issues.

Creation of the .xxx Domain and New gTLDs

Starting in 2010 and 2011, controversies surrounding the roll-out of new generic top level domains (gTLDs) and the addition of the .xxx TLD led some governments to argue for increased government influence on the ICANN policy development process.[24]

.xxx

Since 2000, ICANN has repeatedly considered whether to allow the establishment of a gTLD for adult content. On June 1, 2005, ICANN announced that it had entered into commercial and technical negotiations with a registry company (ICM Registry) to operate a new ".xxx" domain, which would be designated for use by adult websites. With the ICANN Board scheduled to consider final approval of the .xxx domain on August 16, 2005, the Department of Commerce sent a letter to ICANN requesting that adequate additional time be provided to allow ICANN to address the objections of individuals expressing concerns about the impact of pornography on families and children and opposing the creation of a new top level domain devoted to adult content. ICANN's Governmental Advisory Committee (GAC) also requested more time before the final decision.

On March 30, 2007, the ICANN Board voted 9-5 to deny the .xxx domain. ICM Registry subsequently challenged ICANN's decision before an Independent Review Panel (IRP), claiming that ICANN's rejection of ICM's application for a .xxx gTLD was not consistent with ICANN's Articles of Incorporation and Bylaws. On February 19, 2010, a three-person Independent Review Panel ruled primarily in favor of ICM Registry, finding that its application for the .xxx TLD had met the required criteria.

Subsequently, on June 25, 2010, at the ICANN meeting in Brussels, the Board of Directors voted to allow ICM's .xxx application to move forward, and at the December 2010 ICANN meeting, the ICANN Board passed a resolution stating that while "it intends to enter into a registry agreement

---

[23] In the 109th Congress, H.Con.Res. 268 was passed unanimously by the House on November 16, 2005. S.Res. 323 was passed in the Senate by Unanimous Consent on November 18, 2005.

[24] See McCarthy, Kieren, *.nxt*, "Global Internet Governance Fight Looms," September 22, 2011, available at http://news.dot-nxt.com/2011/09/22/internet-governance-fight-looms.

with ICM Registry for the .xxx TLD," the Board would enter into a formal consultation with the Governmental Advisory Committee on areas where the Board's decision was in conflict with GAC advice relating to the ICM application.[25]

While not officially or formally in opposition to the approval of .xxx, the GAC advised ICANN that "there is no active support of the GAC for the introduction of a .xxx TLD" and that "while there are members, which neither endorse nor oppose the introduction of a .xxx TLD, others are emphatically opposed from a public policy perspective to the introduction of an .xxx TLD."[26] The GAC listed a number of specific issues and objections that it wished ICANN to resolve.

A February 2011 letter from ICANN to the GAC acknowledged and responded to areas where approving the .xxx registry agreement with ICM would conflict with GAC advice received by ICANN.[27] The Board acknowledged that ICANN and the GAC were not able to reach a mutually acceptable solution, and ultimately, on March 18, 2011, the Board approved a resolution giving the CEO or General Counsel of ICANN the authority to execute the registry agreement with ICM to establish a .xxx TLD. The vote was nine in favor, three opposed, and four abstentions.

The decision to create a .xxx TLD was not viewed favorably by many governments.[28] In an April 6, 2011, letter to the Department of Commerce, the European Commissioner for the Digital Agenda asked that the introduction of .xxx be delayed.[29] In its response, NTIA said it "share[s] your disappointment that ICANN ignored the clear advice of governments worldwide, including the United States, by approving the new .xxx domain."[30] However, NTIA stated why it would not (and did not) interfere with the addition of .xxx:

> While the Obama Administration does not support ICANN's decision, we respect the multi-stakeholder Internet governance process and do not think that it is in the long-term best interest of the United States or the global Internet community for us unilaterally to reverse the decision. Our goal is to preserve the global Internet, which is a force for innovation, economic growth, and the free flow of information. I agree with you that the Board took its action without the full support of the community and accordingly, I am dedicated to improving the responsiveness of ICANN to all stakeholders, including governments worldwide.[31]

---

[25] ICANN, *Adopted Board Resolutions, Cartegena*, December 10, 2010, available at http://www.icann.org/en/minutes/resolutions-10dec10-en htm#4.

[26] Letter from Chair, Governmental Advisory Committee to ICANN Chairman of the Board, March 16, 2011, available at https://gacweb.icann.org/download/attachments/1540116/20110316+GAC+Advice+on+ xxx.pdf?version=2& modificationDate=1312469527000.

[27] Letter from ICANN to Chair of GAC, February 10, 2011, available at http://icann.org/en/correspondence/jeffrey-to-to-dryden-10feb11-en.pdf.

[28] ICANN must receive formal approval from NTIA for any additions of new gTLDs to the DNS. See Kevin Murphy, "US upset with ICANN over .xxx," *Domain Incite*, March 20, 2011, available at http://domainincite.com/us-upset-with-icann-over-xxx/.

India and Saudi Arabia have stated their intention to block the xxx domain. See "xxx addresses open for business," *The Times of India*, April 19, 2011, available at http://articles.timesofindia.indiatimes.com/2011-04-19/computing/29446429_1_icann-suffix-websites.

[29] Kevin Murphy, "Europe asked US to delay xxx," Domain Incite, May 5, 2011, available at http://domainincite.com/europe-did-ask-the-us-to-delay-xxx/.

[30] Letter from Lawrence Strickling to Neelie Kroes, "Strickling letter to Kroes re: dot-xxx," *.nxt*, April 20, 2011, available at http://news.dot-nxt.com/2011/04/20/strickling-letter-kroes-xxx.

[31] Ibid.

gTLD Expansion

Top Level Domains (TLDs) are the suffixes that appear at the end of an address (after the "dot"). Prior to ICANN's establishment in 1998, the Internet had eight generic top level domains (gTLDs), including .com, .org, .net, and .gov. In 2000 and 2004, ICANN held application rounds for a limited number of new gTLDs—currently there are 22. Some are reserved or restricted to particular types of organizations (e.g., .museum, .gov, .travel) and others are open for registration by anyone (.com, .org, .info). Applicants for new gTLDs are typically commercial entities and non-profit organizations who seek to become ICANN-recognized registries that will establish and operate name servers for their TLD registry, as well as implement a domain name registration process for that particular TLD.

The growth of the Internet and the accompanying growth in demand for domain names have focused the debate on whether and how to further expand the number of gTLDs. Beginning in 2005, ICANN embarked on a long consultative process to develop rules and procedures for introducing and adopting an indefinite number of new gTLDs into the domain name system. A new gTLD can be any word or string of characters that is applied for and approved by ICANN. Between 2008 and 2011, ICANN released seven iterations of its gTLD Applicant Guidebook (essentially the rulebook for how the new gTLD program will be implemented). On June 20, 2011, the ICANN Board of Directors voted to approve the launch of the new gTLD program, under which potentially hundreds of new gTLDs could ultimately be approved by ICANN and introduced into the DNS. Applications for new gTLDs were to be accepted from January 12 through April 12, 2012.

The rollout of new gTLDs was controversial. Advocates (including the domain name industry) argued that a gTLD expansion will provide opportunities for Internet innovation and competition. On the other hand, many trademark holders pointed to possible higher costs and greater difficulties in protecting their trademarks across hundreds of new gTLDs. Similarly, governments expressed concern over intellectual property protections, and along with law enforcement entities, also cited concerns over the added burden of combating various cybercrimes (such as phishing and identity theft) across hundreds of new gTLDs. Throughout ICANN's policy development process, governments, through the Governmental Advisory Committee, advocated for additional intellectual property protections in the new gTLD process. The GAC also argued for more stringent rules that would allow for better law enforcement in the new domain space to better protect consumers. Although changes were made, strong opposition from many trademark holders[32] led to opposition from some parts of the U.S. government towards the end of 2011. For example:

- On December 8, 2011, the Senate Committee on Commerce, Science and Transportation held a hearing on the ICANN's expansion of TLDs. Subsequently, on December 28, 2011, a letter from Senator John Rockefeller, chairman of the Senate Committee on Commerce, Science and Transportation, to the Secretary of Commerce and the Administrator of NTIA, stated his concern that "this expansion of gTLDs, if it proceeds as planned, will have adverse consequences for the millions of American consumers, companies, and non-profit organizations that use the Internet on a daily basis" and that at the hearing, "witnesses speaking

---

[32] The Association of National Advertisers (ANA) has been a leading voice against ICANN's current rollout of the new gTLD program. See ANA webpage, "Say No to ICANN: Generic Top Level Domain Developments," available at http://www.ana.net/content/show/id/icann.

on behalf of more than a hundred companies and non-profit organizations explained that ICANN's current plan for gTLD expansion will likely cause millions of dollars in increased costs related to combating cybersquatting." In the letter, Senator Rockefeller requested that NTIA "should consider asking ICANN to either delay the opening of the application period or to drastically limit the number of new gTLDs it approves next year."[33] A subsequent December 22, 2011, letter to ICANN from Senators Klobuchar and Ayotte also registered concern over the TLD expansion and asked ICANN to further address law enforcement, trademark, and consumer concerns before launching the program.[34]

- On December 14, 2011, the House Committee on Energy and Commerce, Subcommittee on Communications and Technology, held a hearing on ICANN's top level domain program. Subsequently on December 21, 2011, a bipartisan group of Committee Members sent a letter to ICANN requesting that the expansion of the gTLDs be delayed, noting that "many stakeholders are not convinced that ICANN's process has resulted in an acceptable level of protection."[35] The Energy and Commerce Committee members argued that "a short delay will allow interested parties to work with ICANN and offer changes to alleviate many of them, specifically concerns over law enforcement, cost and transparency that were discussed in recent Congressional hearings."[36]

- A December 16, 2011, letter to the Secretary of Commerce from Representative Bob Goodlatte, chairman of the House Subcommittee on Intellectual Property, Competition, and the Internet, and Representative Howard Berman, ranking Member of the House Committee on Foreign Affairs, urged DOC to take all steps necessary to encourage ICANN to undertake further evaluation and review before the gTLD expansion is permitted to occur. The letter asked DOC to determine whether the benefits of the expansion outweigh the costs and risks to consumers, businesses, and the Internet, and that if the program proceeds, that ICANN should initially limit the expansion to a small pilot project which can be evaluated.[37] Previously, the Subcommittee on Intellectual Property, Competition, and the Internet had held a May 4, 2011, hearing on oversight of the gTLD program.

- A December 16, 2011, letter from the Federal Trade Commission (FTC) to ICANN argued that a "rapid, exponential expansion of gTLDs has the potential to magnify both the abuse of the domain name system and the corresponding challenges we encounter in tracking down Internet fraudsters." The FTC urged ICANN to implement the new gTLD program as a pilot program and

---

[33] See "Rockefeller Says Internet Domain Expansion Will Hurt Consumers, Businesses, and Non-Profits—Urges Delay," *Press Release*, Senate Committee on Commerce, Science and Transportation, December 28, 2011, available at http://commerce.senate.gov/public/index.cfm?p=PressReleases.

[34] Letter from Senator Amy Klobuchar and Senator Kelly Ayotte to ICANN, December 22, 2011, available at http://www.icann.org/en/correspondence/klobuchar-ayotte-to-beckstrom-crocker-22dec11-en.pdf.

[35] House Committee on Energy and Commerce, "Committee Urges ICANN to Delay Expansion of Generic Top-Level Domain Program," *Press Release*, December 21, 2011, available at http://energycommerce.house.gov/news/PRArticle.aspx?NewsID=9176.

[36] Ibid.

[37] Letter from Representative Goodlatte and Representative Berman to the Secretary of Commerce, December 16, 2011, available at http://www.icann.org/en/correspondence/goodlatte-berman-to-bryson-16dec11-en.pdf.

---

substantially reduce the number of gTLDs that are introduced in the first application round, strengthen ICANN's contractual compliance program, develop a new ongoing program to monitor consumer issues that arise during the first round of implementing the new gTLD program, conduct an assessment of each new proposed gTLD's risk of consumer harm as part of the evaluation and approval process, and improve the accuracy of WHOIS data, including by imposing a registrant verification requirement. The FTC added that "ICANN should address these issues before it approves any new gTLD applications. If ICANN fails to address these issues responsibly, the introduction of new gTLDs could pose a significant threat to consumers and undermine consumer confidence in the Internet."[38]

- A December 27, 2011, letter to ICANN from the Senate and House Judiciary Committees expressed concerns over the new gTLD program and urged ICANN to "strengthen protections for consumers and trademark holders who risk being harmed by the proliferation of domain names on the web." The letter also urged ICANN to work closely with the law enforcement community "to ensure that the program's rollout does not adversely impact their efforts to fight fraud and abuse on the Internet."[39]

At the December 2011 House and Senate hearings, ICANN stated its intention to proceed with the gTLD expansion as planned. ICANN defended its gTLD program, arguing that the new gTLDs will offer more protections for consumers and trademark holders than current gTLDs; that new gTLDs will provide needed competition, choice, and innovation to the domain name system; and that critics have already had ample opportunity to contribute input during a seven-year deliberative policy development process.[40] Ultimately, ICANN did not delay the initiation of the new gTLD program, and the application window was opened on January 12, 2012, as planned.

Much of the pressure on ICANN to delay the new gTLD program was directed at NTIA, given NTIA's unique relationship with ICANN. At both the December 2011 Senate and House hearings, NTIA expressed support for ICANN's planned rollout of the TLD expansion program, arguing that national governments have been able to address intellectual property, law enforcement, and consumer concerns through the Governmental Advisory Committee (GAC):

> NTIA believes that ICANN improved the new gTLD program by incorporating a significant number of proposals from the GAC. ICANN's new gTLD program also now provides law enforcement and consumer protection authorities with significantly more tools than those available in existing gTLDs to address malicious conduct. The fact that not all of the GAC's

---

[38] Letter from FTC to ICANN, December 16, 2011, available at http://www.ftc.gov/os/closings/publicltrs/111216letter-to-icann.pdf.

[39] Letter from the Chairmen and Ranking Members of the Senate and House Judiciary Committees to Rod Beckstrom, CEO, ICANN, December 27, 2011, available at http://www.icann.org/en/correspondence/leahy-to-beckstrom-27dec11-en.pdf.

[40] Testimony of Kurt Pritz, Senior Vice President, ICANN, before the House Committee on Energy and Commerce, Subcommittee on Communications and Technology, December 14, 2011, available at http://republicans.energycommerce.house.gov/Media/file/Hearings/Telecom/121411/Pritz.pdf. The gTLD expansion is also strongly supported by many in the Internet and domain name industry, see letter to Senator Rockefeller and Senator Hutchison at http://news.dot-nxt.com/sites/news.dot-nxt.com/files/gtld-industry-to-congress-gtlds-8dec11.pdf.

proposals were adopted as originally offered does not represent a failure of the process or a setback to governments; rather, it reflects the reality of a multi-stakeholder model.[41]

While NTIA stated that it would continue to monitor progress and push for necessary changes to ICANN's TLD expansion program, a key aspect of NTIA's argument for supporting ICANN's planned rollout was to preserve the integrity of the multistakeholder Internet governance process:

> NTIA is dedicated to maintaining an open, global Internet that remains a valuable tool for economic growth, innovation, and the free flow of information, goods, and services online. We believe the best way to achieve this goal is to continue to actively support and participate in multi-stakeholder Internet governance processes such as ICANN. This is in stark contrast to some countries that are actively seeking to move Internet policy to the United Nations. If we are to combat the proposals put forward by others, we need to ensure that our multi-stakeholder institutions have provided a meaningful role for governments as stakeholders. NTIA believes that the strength of the multi-stakeholder approach to Internet policy-making is that it allows for speed, flexibility, and decentralized problem-solving and stands in stark contrast to a more traditional, top-down regulatory model characterized by rigid processes, political capture by incumbents, and in so many cases, impasse or stalemate.[42]

On January 3, 2012, NTIA sent ICANN a letter concerning implementation of the new gTLD program.[43] While NTIA recognized that the program "is the product of a six-year international multistakeholder process" and that NTIA does "not seek to interfere with the decisions and compromises reached during that process," NTIA urged ICANN to consider implementing measures to address many of the criticisms raised. Such measures would address concerns of trademark holders, law enforcement, and consumer protection. NTIA also asked ICANN to assess (after the initial application window closes and the list of prospective new gTLDs is known) whether there is a need to phase in the introduction of new gTLDs, and whether additional trademark protection measures need to be taken.

NTIA concluded its letter as follows:

> How ICANN handles the new gTLD program will, for many, be a litmus test of the viability of this approach. For its part, NTIA is committed to continuing to be an active member of the GAC and working with stakeholders to mitigate any unintended consequences of the new gTLD program.[44]

On June 13, 2012, ICANN announced it had received 1,930 applications for new gTLDs,[45] and ICANN has now moved into the evaluation phase; ICANN will decide whether or not to accept each of the 1,930 new gTLD applications. With the first round application period concluded, there remain significant issues in play as the new gTLD program goes forward. First, ICANN has

---

[41] Testimony of Fiona M. Alexander, Associate Administrator, NTIA, before the House Committee on Energy and Commerce, Subcommittee on Communications and Technology, December 14, 2011, available at http://www.ntia.doc.gov/speechtestimony/2011/testimony-associate-administrator-alexander-icann-s-top-level-domain-name-progr.

[42] Ibid.

[43] Letter from Lawrence Strickling, Assistant Secretary for Communications and Information, U.S. Department of Commerce, to ICANN, January 3, 2012, available at http://www.ntia.doc.gov/other-publication/2012/ntia-letter-regarding-gtld-program.

[44] Ibid.

[45] A complete list of new gTLD applications is provided at http://newgtlds.icann.org/en/program-status/application-results/strings-1200utc-13jun12-en.

stated that a second and subsequent round will take place, and that changes to the application and evaluation process will be made such that a "systemized manner of applying for gTLDs be developed in the long term."[46] ICANN's goal is to begin the second application round "within one year of the close of the application submission period for the initial round."[47] Thus, many observers are eager to see what changes may be made in the second round.

Second, when the new gTLDs go "live," many stakeholders are concerned that various forms of domain name abuse (e.g., trademark infringement, consumer fraud, malicious behavior, etc.) could manifest itself within the hundreds of new gTLD domain spaces. Thus, the effectiveness of ICANN's approach to addressing such issues as intellectual property protection of second level domain names and mitigating unlawful behavior in the domain name space will be of interest as the new gTLD program goes forward.

With respect to the new gTLD program, the GAC provides advice to the ICANN Board on any first round applications the GAC considers problematic. GAC advice can take three forms:

> I. The GAC advises ICANN that it is the consensus of the GAC that a particular application should not proceed. This will create a strong presumption for the ICANN Board that the application should not be approved.

> II. The GAC advises ICANN that there are concerns about a particular application "dot-example." The ICANN Board is expected to enter into dialogue with the GAC to understand the scope of concerns. The ICANN Board is also expected to provide a rationale for its decision.

> III. The GAC advises ICANN that an application should not proceed unless remediated. This will raise a strong presumption for the Board that the application should not proceed unless there is a remediation method available in the Guidebook (such as securing the approval of one or more governments), that is implemented by the applicant.[48]

The GAC also issues Early Warnings to the ICANN Board in the event that any GAC member finds an application problematic for any reason. An Early Warning is an indication that a formal GAC objection is possible (either through the GAC advice process or through the formal objection process). Applicants are notified of an Early Warning against their application and given the opportunity to address the concerns or to withdraw the application (thereby qualifying for a partial refund of the application fee).

Proposed Models for Internet Governance

As discussed above, ICANN is a working example of a multistakeholder model of Internet governance, whereby a bottom-up collaborative process is used to provide Internet stakeholders with access to the policymaking process. Support for the multistakeholder model of Internet governance is reflected in international organizations such as the Organisation for Economic Co-operation and Development (OECD) and the Group of Eight (G8). For example, the OECD's

---

[46] ICANN, *New gTLD Applicant Guidebook*, June 4, 2012, Module 1, pp. 1-21, available at http://newgtlds.icann.org/en/applicants/agb.

[47] Ibid.

[48] Ibid., Module 3, p. 3-3.

Communiqué on Principles for Internet Policy-Making cites multistakeholderism as a central tenet of Internet governance:

> In particular, continued support is needed for the multi-stakeholder environment, which has underpinned the process of Internet governance and the management of critical Internet resources (such as naming and numbering resources) and these various stakeholders should continue to fully play a role in this framework. Governments should also work in multi-stakeholder environments to achieve international public policy goals and strengthen international co-operation in Internet governance.[49]

Similarly, at the G8 Summit of Deauville on May 26-27, 2011, the G8 issued a declaration on its renewed commitment for freedom and democracy that contained a new section on the Internet. Support for a multistakeholder model for Internet governance with a significant national government role was made explicit:

> As we support the multi-stakeholder model of Internet governance, we call upon all stakeholders to contribute to enhanced cooperation within and between all international fora dealing with the governance of the Internet. In this regard, flexibility and transparency have to be maintained in order to adapt to the fast pace of technological and business developments and uses. Governments have a key role to play in this model.[50]

As discussed above, in 2005, the World Summit on the Information Society (WSIS) considered four models of Internet governance, of which three would have involved an intergovernmental body to oversee the Internet and the domain name system. While the WSIS ultimately decided not to pursue an intergovernmental model in 2005, some nations have again advocated an intergovernmental approach for Internet governance. For example:

- India, Brazil, and South Africa (referred to as IBSA) proposed that "an appropriate body is urgently required in the U.N. system to coordinate and evolve coherent and integrated global public policies pertaining to the Internet." The IBSA proposed body would "integrate and oversee the bodies responsible for technical and operational functioning of the Internet, including global standards setting."[51]

- In order to implement the major aspects of the IBSA proposal, the government of India proposed (in the U.N. General Assembly) the establishment of a new institutional mechanism in the United Nations for global Internet-related policies, to be called the United Nations Committee for Internet-Related Policies (CIRP). CIRP would be comprised of 50 member states chosen on the basis of equitable geographical representation. The Internet Governance Forum (IGF) and four advisory stakeholder groups would provide input to CIRP, which would report directly to the General Assembly and present recommendations for consideration,

---

[49] Organisation for Economic Co-operation and Development, OECD High Level Meeting, The Internet Economy: Generating Innovation and Growth, *Communique on Principles for Internet Policy-Making*, June 28-29, 2011, p. 4, available at http://www.oecd.org/dataoecd/33/12/48387430.pdf.

[50] G8 Declaration, Renewed Commitment for Freedom and Democracy, G8 Summit of Deauville, May 26-27, 2011, available at http://www.g20-g8.com/g8-g20/g8/english/live/news/renewed-commitment-for-freedom-and-democracy.1314.html.

[51] IBSA Multistakeholder meeting on Global Internet Governance, *Recommendations*, September 1-2, 2011 at Rio de Janeiro, Brazil, available at http://www.culturalivre.org.br/artigos/IBSA_recommendations_Internet_Governance.pdf.

adoption, and dissemination among all relevant intergovernmental bodies and international organizations.[52]

- Another group of nations, including China and the Russian Federation, proposed a voluntary "International Code of Conduct for Information Security," for further discussion in the U.N. General Assembly. The Code includes language that promotes the establishment of a multilateral, transparent, and democratic international management system to ensure an equitable distribution of resources, facilitate access for all, and ensure a stable and secure functioning of the Internet.[53]

Thus, governments such as the United States and the European Union support ICANN's multistakeholder model, while at the same time advocating increased governmental influence within that model.[54] By contrast, other nations support an expanded role for an intergovernmental model of Internet governance. The debate has been summarized by NTIA as follows:

> By engaging all interested parties, multistakeholder processes encourage broader and more creative problem solving, which is essential when markets and technology are changing as rapidly as they are. They promote speedier, more flexible decision making than is common under traditional, top-down regulatory models which can too easily fall prey to rigid procedures, bureaucracy, and stalemate. But there is a challenge emerging to this model in parts of the world.... Some nations appear to prefer an Internet managed and controlled by nation-states. In December 2012, the U.S. will participate in the ITU's World Conference on International Telecommunications (WCIT). This treaty negotiation will conduct a review of the International Telecommunication Regulations (ITRs), the general principles which relate to traditional international voice telecommunication services. We expect that some states will attempt to rewrite the regulation in a manner that would exclude the contributions of multi-stakeholder organizations and instead provide for heavy-handed governmental control of the Internet, including provisions for cybersecurity and granular operational and technical requirements for private industry. We do not support any of these elements. It is critical that we work with the private sector on outreach to countries to promote the multi-stakeholder model as a credible alternative.[55]

---

[52] The CIRP proposal is available at http://igfwatch.org/discussion-board/indias-proposal-for-a-un-committee-for-internet-related-policies-cirp.

[53] United Nations General Assembly, Sixty-sixth session, Item 93 of the provisional agenda, Developments in the field of information and telecommunications in the context of international security, "Letter dated 12 September 2011 from the Permanent Representatives of China, the Russian Federation, Tajikistan, and Uzbekistan to the United Nations addressed to the Secretary-General," September 14, 2011, A/66/359, available at http://blog.internetgovernance.org/pdf/UN-infosec-code.pdf.

[54] The European Commission has been a particularly strong voice in favor of significantly increasing GAC influence on the ICANN policy process. See Kieren McCarthy, "European Commission calls for greater government control over Internet," .nxt, August 31, 2011, available at http://news.dot-nxt.com/2011/08/31/ec-greater-government-control.

[55] Remarks by Lawrence Strickling, Assistant Secretary of Commerce for Communications and Information, National Telecommunications and Information Administration, Department of Commerce, before the PLI/FCBA Telecommunications Policy & Regulation Institute, Washington, DC, December 8, 2011, available at http://www.ntia.doc.gov/speechtestimony/2011/remarks-assistant-secretary-strickling-practising-law-institutes-29th-annual-te.

World Conference on International Telecommunications (WCIT)

The World Conference on International Telecommunications (WCIT) was held in Dubai on December 3-14, 2012. Convened by the International Telecommunications Union (the ITU, an agency within the United Nations), the WCIT was a formal meeting of the world's national governments held in order to revise the International Telecommunications Regulations (ITRs). The ITRs, previously revised in 1988, serve as a global treaty outlining the principles which govern the way international telecommunications traffic is handled.

Because the existing 24-year-old ITRs predated the Internet, one of the key policy questions in the WCIT was how and to what extent the updated ITRs should address Internet traffic and Internet governance. The Administration and Congress took the position that the new ITRs should continue to address only traditional international telecommunications traffic, that a multistakeholder model of Internet governance (such as ICANN) should continue, and that the ITU should not take any action that could extend its jurisdiction or authority over the Internet.

As the WCIT approached, concerns heightened in the 112th Congress that the WCIT might potentially provide a forum leading to an increased level of intergovernmental control over the Internet. On May 31, 2012, the House Committee on Energy and Commerce, Subcommittee on Communications and Technology, held a hearing entitled, "International Proposals to Regulate the Internet."[56] To accompany the hearing, H.Con.Res. 127 was introduced by Representative Bono Mack expressing the sense of Congress regarding actions to preserve and advance the multistakeholder governance model. Specifically, H.Con.Res. 127 expressed the sense of Congress that the Administration "should continue working to implement the position of the United States on Internet governance that clearly articulates the consistent and unequivocal policy of the United States to promote a global Internet free from government control and preserve and advance the successful multistakeholder model that governs the Internet today." H.Con.Res. 127 was passed unanimously by the House (414-0) on August 2, 2012.

A similar resolution, S.Con.Res. 50, was introduced into the Senate by Senator Rubio on June 27, 2012, and referred to the Committee on Foreign Relations. The Senate resolution expressed the sense of Congress "that the Secretary of State, in consultation with the Secretary of Commerce, should continue working to implement the position of the United States on Internet governance that clearly articulates the consistent and unequivocal policy of the United States to promote a global Internet free from government control and preserve and advance the successful multistakeholder model that governs the Internet today." S.Con.Res. 50 was passed by the Senate by unanimous consent on September 22, 2012. On December 5, 2012—shortly after the WCIT had begun in Dubai—the House unanimously passed S.Con.Res. 50 by a vote of 397-0.

During the WCIT, a revision to the ITRs was proposed and supported by Russia, China, Saudi Arabia, Algeria, and Sudan that sought to explicitly extend ITR jurisdiction over Internet traffic, infrastructure, and governance. Specifically, the proposal stated that "Member States shall have the sovereign right to establish and implement public policy, including international policy, on matters of Internet governance."[57] The proposal also included an article establishing the right of Member States to manage Internet numbering, naming, addressing, and identification resources.

---

[56] Available at http://energycommerce.house.gov/hearings/hearingdetail.aspx?NewsID=9543.

[57] See Article 3A, "Proposals for the Work of the Conference," available at http://files.wcitleaks.org/public/Merged%20UAE%208081212.pdf.

The proposal was subsequently withdrawn. However, as an intended compromise, the ITU adopted a nonbinding resolution (Resolution 3, attached to the final ITR text) entitled, "To Foster an enabling environment for the greater growth of the Internet." Resolution 3 includes language stating "all governments should have an equal role and responsibility for international Internet governance" and invites Member States to "elaborate on their respective positions on international Internet-related technical, development and public policy issues within the mandate of ITU at various ITU forums."[58]

Because of the inclusion of Resolution 3, along with other features of the final ITR text (such as new ITU articles related to spam and cybersecurity), the United States declined to sign the treaty. The leader of the U.S. delegation stated the following:

> The Internet has given the world unimaginable economic and social benefits during these past 24 years—all without UN regulation. We candidly cannot support an ITU treaty that is inconsistent with a multi-stakeholder model of Internet governance. As the ITU has stated, this conference was never meant to focus on internet issues; however, today we are in a situation where we still have text and resolutions that cover issues on spam and also provisions on internet governance. These past two weeks, we have of course made good progress and shown a willingness to negotiate on a variety of telecommunications policy issues, such as roaming and settlement rates, but the United States continues to believe that internet policy must be multi-stakeholder driven. Internet policy should not be determined by member states but by citizens, communities, and broader society, and such consultation from the private sector and civil society is paramount. This has not happened here.[59]

Of the 144 eligible members of the ITU, 89 nations signed the treaty, while 55 either chose not to sign (such as the United States) or remain undecided.[60]

While the WCIT in Dubai is concluded, the international debate over Internet governance is expected to continue in future intergovernmental telecommunications meetings and conferences. The 113th Congress is overseeing and supporting the U.S. government's continuing efforts to resist international attempts to exert control over Internet governance. On February 5, 2013, the House Committee on Energy and Commerce, Subcommittee on Communications and Technology, held a hearing entitled "Fighting for Internet Freedom: Dubai and Beyond." The hearing was held jointly with the House Committee on Foreign Affairs, Subcommittee on Terrorism, Nonproliferation, and Trade and the Subcommittee on Africa, Global Health, Global Human Rights, and International Organizations.

On April 16, 2013, H.R. 1580, a bill "To Affirm the Policy of the United States Regarding Internet Governance," was introduced by Representative Walden. Using language similar to the WCIT-related congressional resolutions passed by the 112th Congress (S.Con.Res. 50 and H.Con.Res. 127), H.R. 1580 states that "It is the policy of the United States to preserve and advance the successful multistakeholder model that governs the Internet." On May 14, 2013, H.R. 1580 was passed unanimously (413-0) by the House of Representatives.

---

[58] International Telecommunications Union, *Final Acts*, World Conference on International Telecommunications, Dubai, 2012, Resolution 3, p. 20, available at http://www.itu.int/en/wcit-12/Documents/final-acts-wcit-12.pdf.

[59] Statement delivered by Ambassador Terry Kramer from the floor of the WCIT, December 13, 2012. U.S. Department of State, *Press Release*, "U.S. Intervention at the World Conference on International Telecommunications," December 13, 2012, available at http://www.state.gov/r/pa/prs/ps/2012/12/202037 htm.

[60] The official ITU list of signatories and non-signatories is at http://www.itu.int/osg/wcit-12/highlights/signatories html.

Montevideo Statement on the Future of Internet Cooperation

In October 2013, the President of ICANN and the leaders of other major organizations responsible for globally coordinating Internet technical infrastructure[61] met in Montevideo, Uruguay, and released a statement calling for strengthening the current mechanisms for global multistakeholder Internet cooperation. Their recommendations included the following:

- They reinforced the importance of globally coherent Internet operations, and warned against Internet fragmentation at a national level. They expressed strong concern over the undermining of the trust and confidence of Internet users globally due to recent revelations of pervasive monitoring and surveillance.

- They identified the need for ongoing effort to address Internet Governance challenges, and agreed to catalyze community-wide efforts towards the evolution of global multistakeholder Internet cooperation.

- They called for accelerating the globalization of ICANN and IANA functions, towards an environment in which all stakeholders, including all governments, participate on an equal footing.[62]

NETmundial

The day after the Montevideo Statement was released, the President of ICANN met with the President of Brazil, who announced plans to hold an international Internet governance summit in April 2014 that would include representatives from government, industry, civil society, and academia. NETmundial, which was described as a "global multistakeholder meeting on the future of Internet governance," was held on April 23-24, 2014, in Sao Paulo, Brazil.[63] The meeting was open to all interested stakeholders, and was intended to "focus on crafting Internet governance principles and proposing a roadmap for the further evolution of the Internet governance ecosystem."[64]

The outcome of NETmundial produced a nonbinding "NETmundial Multistakeholder Statement"[65] that set forth general Internet governance principles and identified issues to be discussed at future meetings on the future evolution of Internet governance. According to the U.S. government delegation at NETmundial, the meeting outcome reaffirmed the multistakeholder model of Internet governance, endorsed the transition of the U.S. government's stewardship role of IANA functions to the global multistakeholder community, emphasized the importance of strengthening and expanding upon the mandate of the Internet Governance Forum, and underscored the importance of human rights in the implementation of a free and open Internet.[66]

---

[61] The Internet Society, World Wide Web Consortium, Internet Engineering Task Force, Internet Architecture Board, and all five of the regional Internet address registries.

[62] Full statement is available at http://www.icann.org/en/news/announcements/announcement-07oct13-en htm.

[63] Further information on NETmundial is available at http://netmundial.br/.

[64] Ibid.

[65] Available at http://netmundial.br/wp-content/uploads/2014/04/NETmundial-Multistakeholder-Document.pdf.

[66] United States Diplomatic Mission to Brazil, "Official Statement by the USG Delegation to NETmundial," April 25, 2014, available at http://brazil.usembassy.gov/statementusgdeletationnetmundial html.

Issues for Congress

Congress plays an important role overseeing NTIA's stewardship of the domain name system and ICANN. The House Committee on Energy and Commerce and the Senate Committee on Commerce, Science, and Transportation have held numerous oversight hearings exploring ICANN's performance in general, as well as specific DNS issues that arise (e.g., the proposed gTLD expansion). Additionally, other committees, such as the House and Senate Judiciary Committees, maintain an interest in the DNS as it affects Internet policy issues such as intellectual property, privacy, and cybercrime. Since 1997, congressional committees have held 33 hearings on the DNS and ICANN.[67]

Congress is likely to closely examine NTIA's March 14, 2014, proposed transitioning of its authority over ICANN and the DNS to a wholly multistakeholder-driven entity. Congress will likely consider whether the proposed transition is in the best interest of the United States and in the best interest of the Internet. As a transition plan is developed by ICANN and the Internet community, Congress will likely monitor and evaluate that plan, and seek assurances that a DNS free of U.S. government stewardship will remain stable, secure, resilient, and open. As part of its examination, Congress will likely continue assessing to what extent ongoing and future intergovernmental telecommunications conferences constitute an opportunity for some nations to increase intergovernmental control over the Internet, and how effectively NTIA and other government agencies (such as the State Department) are working to counteract that threat.

Finally, the ongoing debate over Internet governance will likely have a significant impact on how other aspects of the Internet may be governed in the future, especially in such areas as intellectual property, privacy, law enforcement, Internet free speech, and cybersecurity. Looking forward, the institutional nature of Internet governance could have far-reaching implications on important policy decisions that will likely shape the future evolution of the Internet.

---

[67] For a complete list, see the Appendix in CRS Report 97-868, *Internet Domain Names: Background and Policy Issues*, by Lennard G. Kruger.

Appendix. ICANN Basics

ICANN is a not-for-profit public benefit corporation headquartered in Marina del Rey, CA, and incorporated under the laws of the state of California. ICANN is organized under the California Nonprofit Public Benefit Law for charitable and public purposes, and as such, is subject to legal oversight by the California attorney general. ICANN has been granted tax-exempt status by the federal government and the state of California.[68]

ICANN's organizational structure consists of a Board of Directors (BOD) advised by a network of supporting organizations and advisory committees that represent various Internet constituencies and interests (see **Figure A-1**). Policies are developed and issues are researched by these subgroups, who in turn advise the Board of Directors, which is responsible for making all final policy and operational decisions. The Board of Directors consists of 16 international and geographically diverse members, composed of one president, eight members selected by a Nominating Committee, two selected by the Generic Names Supporting Organization, two selected by the Address Supporting Organization, two selected by the Country-Code Names Supporting Organization, and one selected by the At-Large Advisory Committee. Additionally, there are five non-voting liaisons representing other advisory committees.

The explosive growth of the Internet and domain name registration, along with increasing responsibilities in managing and operating the DNS, has led to marked growth of the ICANN budget, from revenues of about $6 million and a staff of 14 in 2000, to revenues of $239 million and a staff of 178 forecast in 2013.[69] ICANN has been traditionally funded primarily through fees paid to ICANN by registrars and registry operators. Registrars are companies (e.g., GoDaddy, Google, Network Solutions) with which consumers register domain names.[70] Registry operators are companies and organizations that operate and administer the master database of all domain names registered in each top level domain (for example VeriSign, Inc. operates .com and .net, Public Interest Registry operates .org, and Neustar, Inc. operates .biz).[71]

Additionally, the collection of fees from the new generic top level domain (gTLD) program could contribute to an unprecedented level of revenue for ICANN in the years to come. For example, ICANN forecasts revenues of $162 million from the new gTLD application fees in 2013, which is twice the amount of traditional revenues from all other sources.[72]

---

[68] ICANN, *2008 Annual Report*, December 31, 2008, p. 24, available at http://www.icann.org/en/annualreport/annual-report-2008-en.pdf.

[69] ICANN Board Meeting, *FY14 Budget Approval*, August 22, 2013, available at http://www.icann.org/en/about/financials/adopted-opplan-budget-fy14-22aug13-en.pdf.

[70] A list of ICANN-accredited registrars is available at http://www.icann.org/en/registries/agreements htm.

[71] A list of current agreements between ICANN and registry operators is available at http://www.icann.org/en/registries/agreements htm.

[72] *FY14 Budget Approval*, p. 4.

Figure A-1. Organizational Structure of ICANN

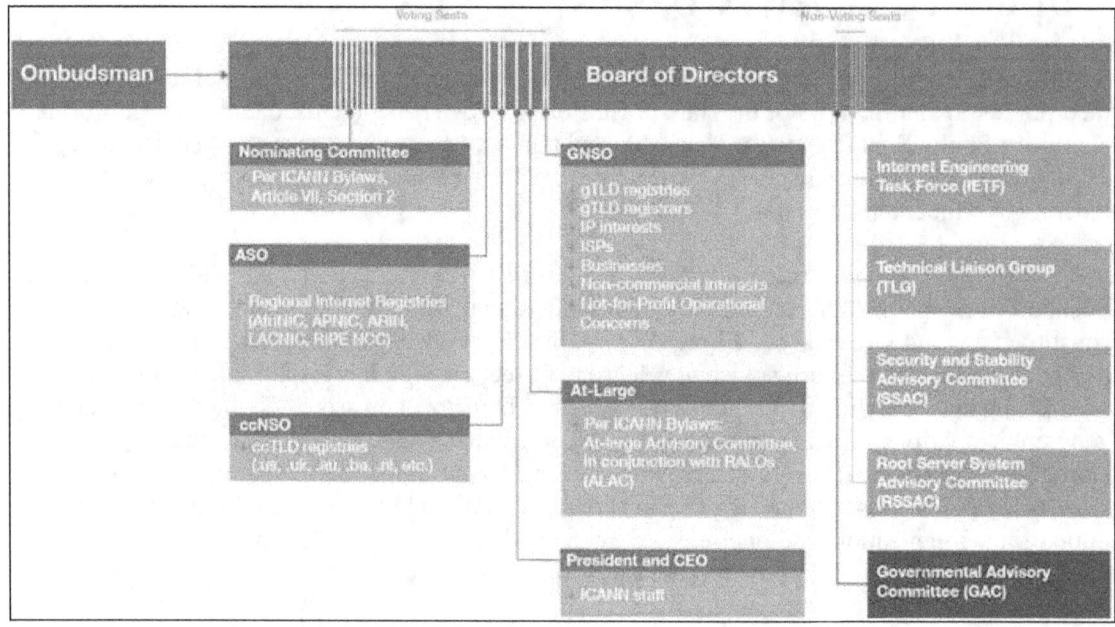

Source: ICANN; http://www.icann.org/en/groups/chart.

Author Contact Information

Lennard G. Kruger
Specialist in Science and Technology Policy
lkruger@crs.loc.gov, 7-7070